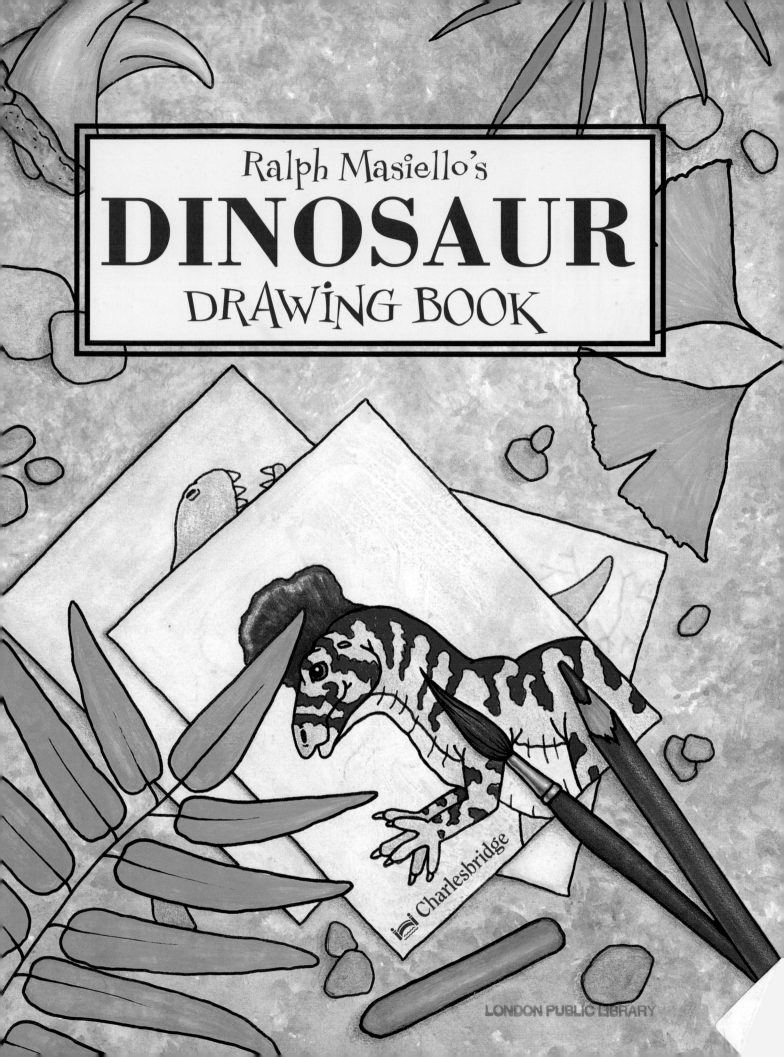

Ralph Masiello's
DINOSAUR
DRAWING BOOK

Charlesbridge

For Stephanie, who brings order to my chaos—R. M.

Also in this series:
Ralph Masiello's Bug Drawing Book
Ralph Masiello's Ocean Drawing Book

Other books illustrated by Ralph Masiello:
The Dinosaur Alphabet Book
The Extinct Alphabet Book
The Flag We Love
The Frog Alphabet Book
The Icky Bug Alphabet Book
The Icky Bug Counting Book
The Skull Alphabet Book
The Yucky Reptile Alphabet Book
Cuenta los insectos

Published by Charlesbridge
85 Main Street
Watertown, MA 02472
(617) 926-0329
www.charlesbridge.com

Library of Congress Cataloging-in-Publication Data
Masiello, Ralph.
    [Dinosaur drawing book]
    Ralph Masiello's dinosaur drawing book.
    p. cm.
    ISBN-13: 978-1-57091-527-7; ISBN-10: 1-57091-527-X (reinforced for library use)
    ISBN-13: 978-1-57091-528-4; ISBN-10: 1-57091-528-8 (softcover)
1. Dinosaurs in art—Juvenile literature.
2. Drawing—Technique—Juvenile literature. I. Title.
NC780.5.M37 2005
743.6—dc22   2004018935

Printed in China
(hc) 10 9 8 7 6 5 4 3 2 1
(sc) 10 9 8 7 6 5 4 3 2

Illustrations done in mixed media
Display type set in Couchlover, designed by Chank, Minneapolis, Minnesota;
       text type set in Goudy
Color separated, printed, and bound by Jade Productions
Production supervision by Brian G. Walker
Designed by Susan Mallory Sherman

Hello, Fellow Artists!

My name is Ralph Masiello, and I'm an illustrator. I've illustrated many books for kids, including *The Icky Bug Alphabet Book, The Flag We Love,* and *The Dinosaur Alphabet Book.* In this book I'll show you simple ways to draw some of the most incredible creatures that ever roamed the planet: DINOSAURS! Dinosaurs lived on the earth for 150 million years, and the last of them died out nearly 65 million years ago. No human has ever seen one alive, but maybe, with practice and creativity, you can bring dinosaurs back to life through your drawings. Follow the red steps to create these fascinating creatures and their surroundings. Then color in your drawings using whichever art tool you like best. You'll find blue extra challenge steps in boxes throughout the book. Remember, the more you practice, the better your drawings become. So practice, practice, practice, and most importantly, have fun!

Happy drawing,

Ralph

Choose your tools

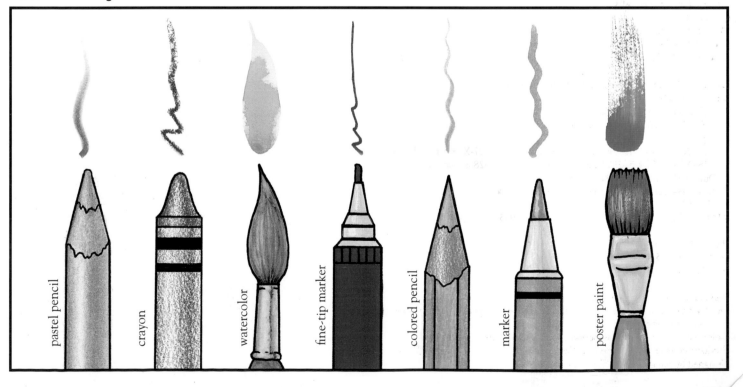

pastel pencil

crayon

watercolor

fine-tip marker

colored pencil

marker

poster paint

Dinosaur Eggs

Hatching Eggs

Let's get cracking!

crayon

Claws

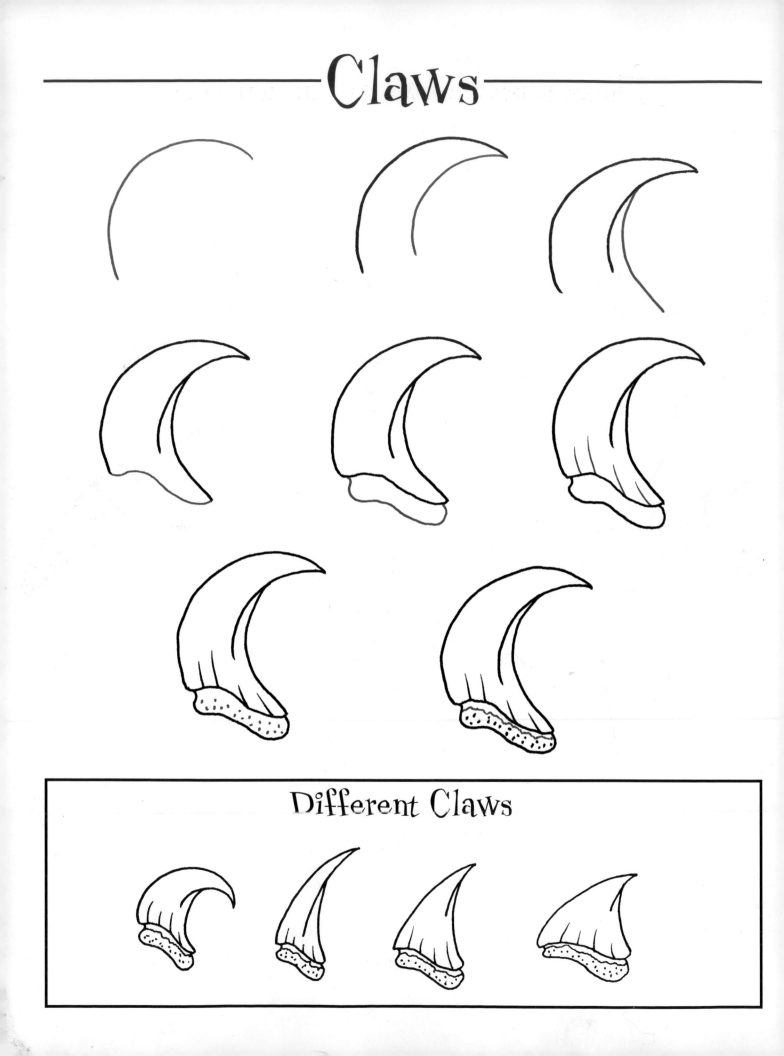

Different Claws

These raptor claws are actual size.

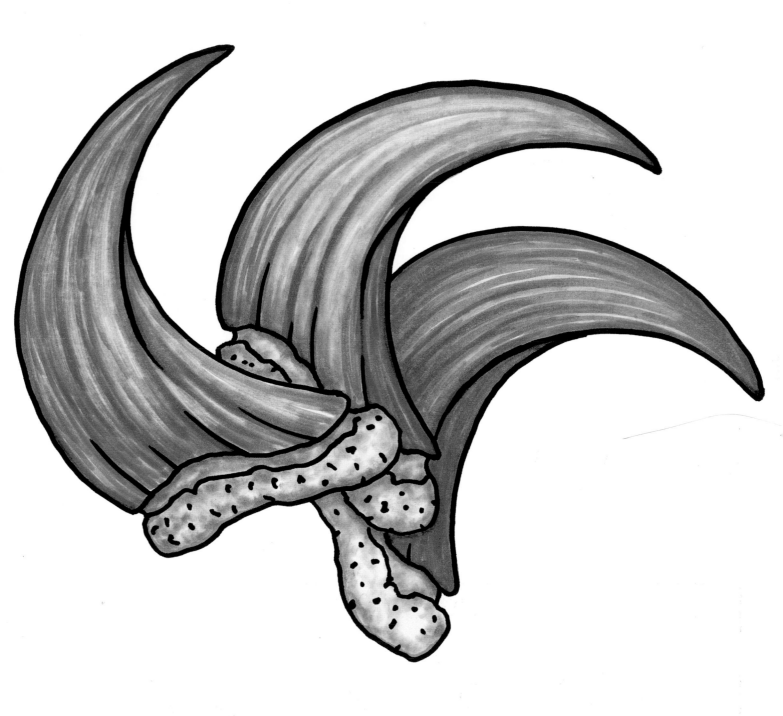

marker

Fossil Skull

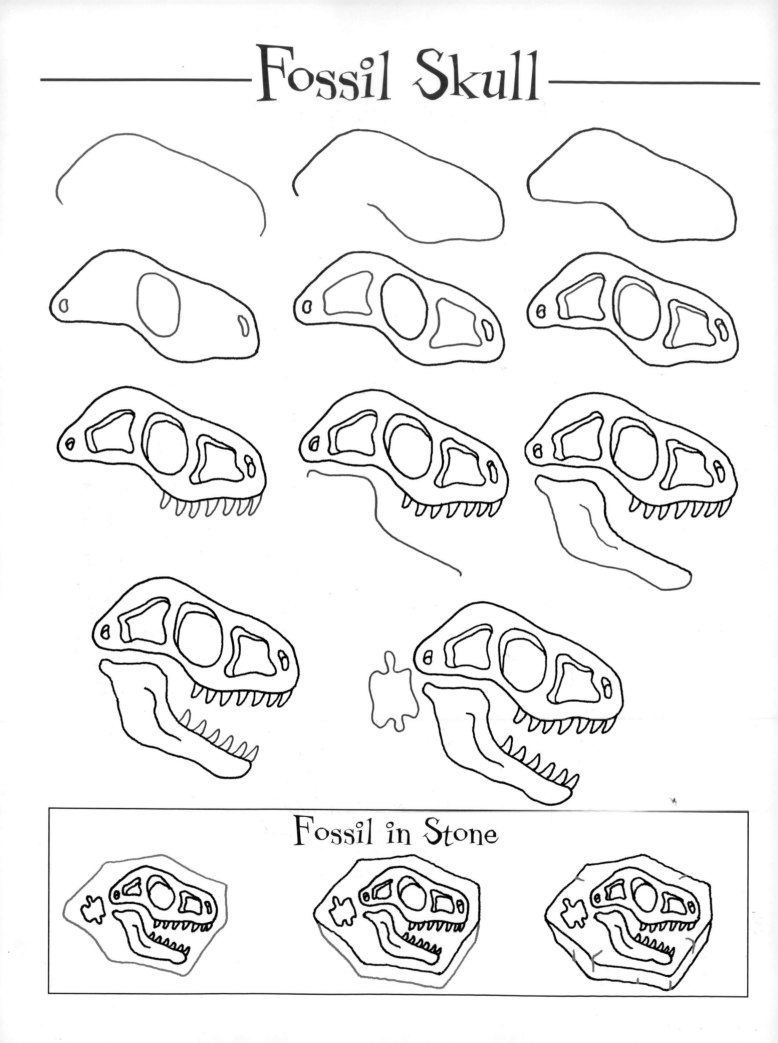

Fossil in Stone

Finding fossils is fun!

poster paint

Prehistoric Plants

Fern Ginkgo Cycad

Clouds and Mountains

Clouds

Mountains

Hills

Overlapping Clouds

Mountains and Hills

Triceratops

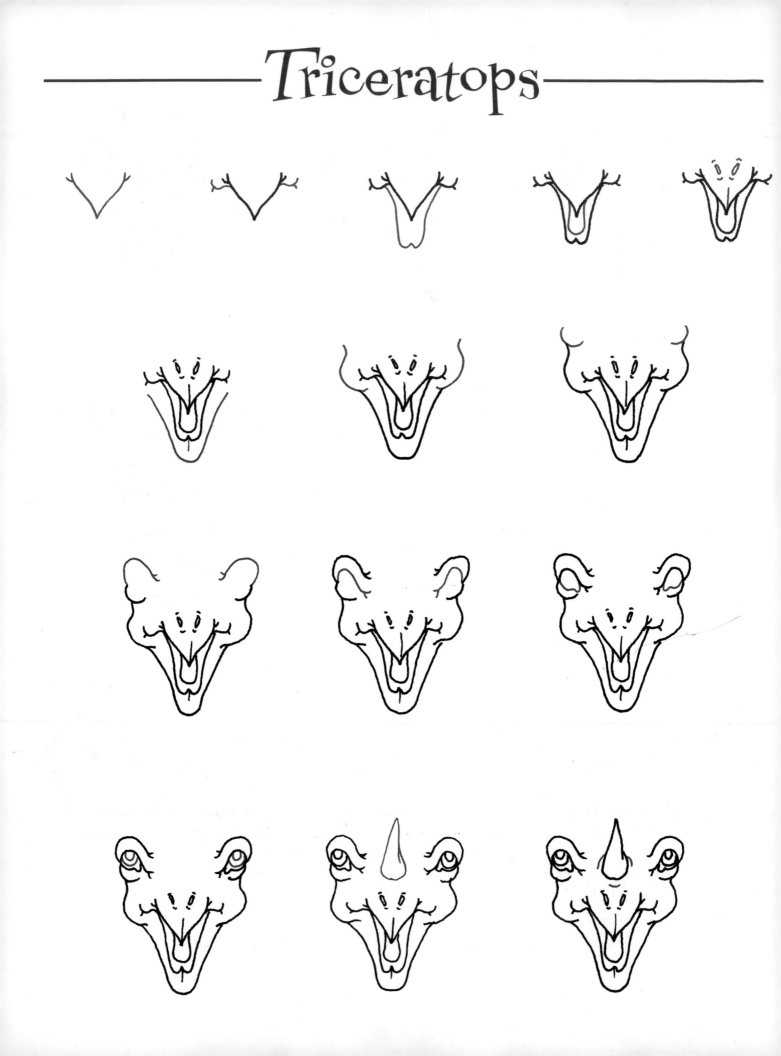

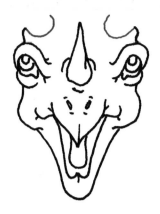

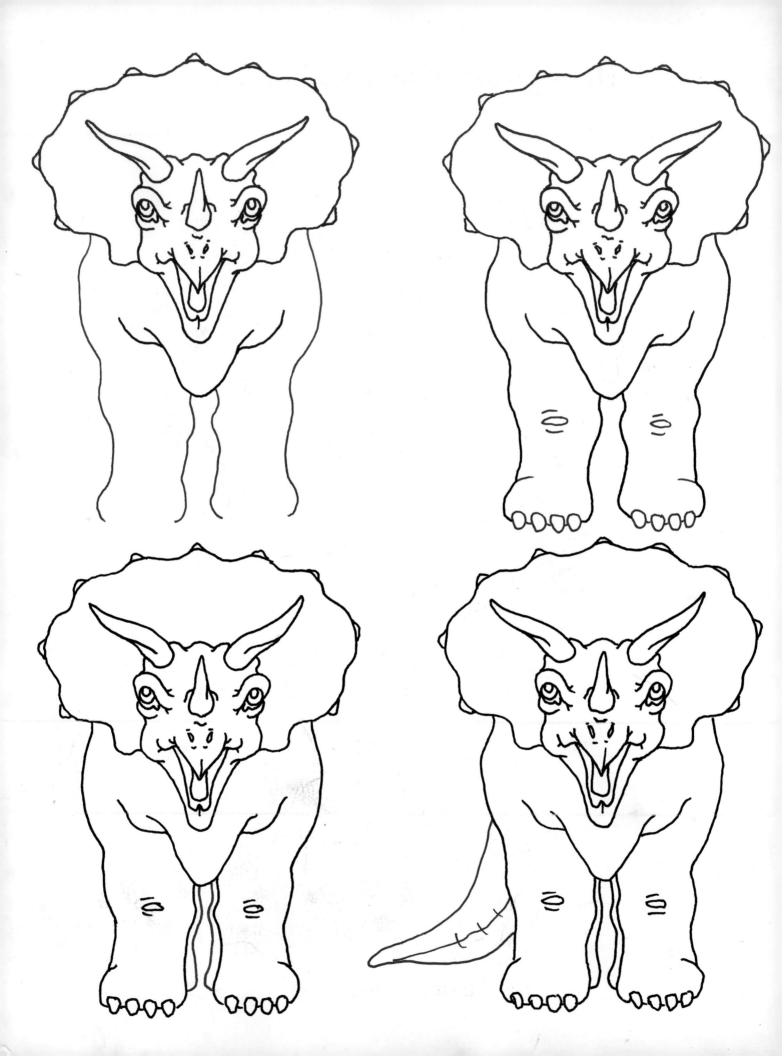

Here's looking at you, kid. . . .

marker and poster paint

Stegosaurus

Realistic Eye

Can I have a back rub?

watercolor

Pterodactyl

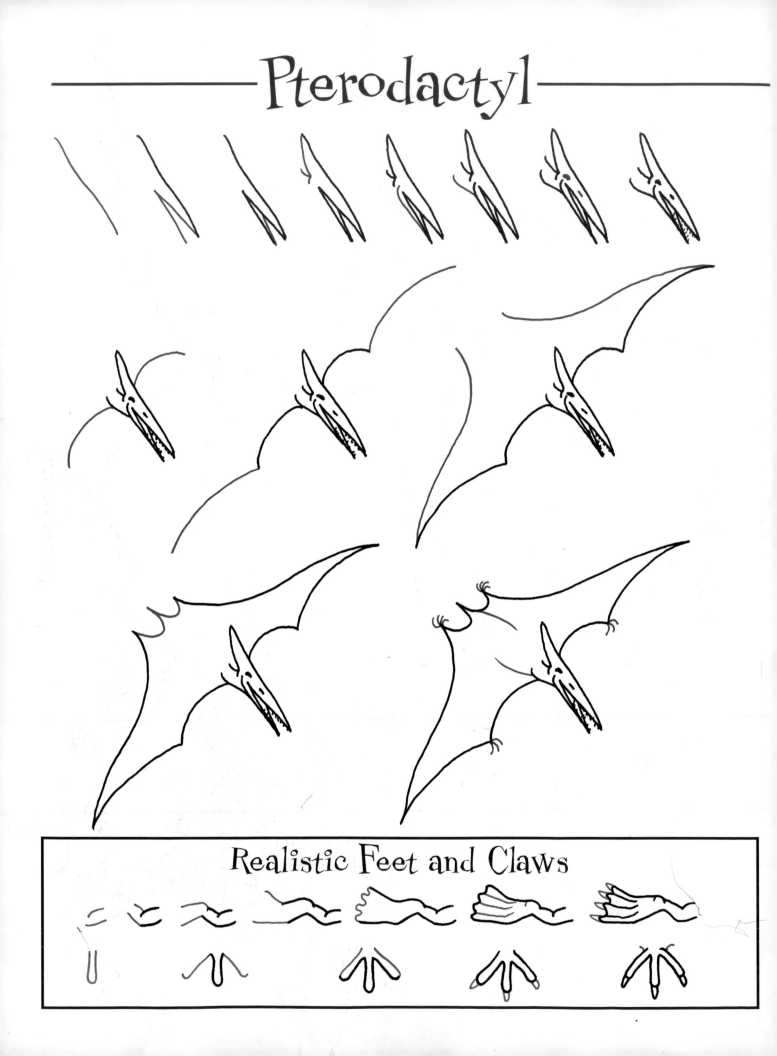

Realistic Feet and Claws

-Duck-billed Dinosaur Head-

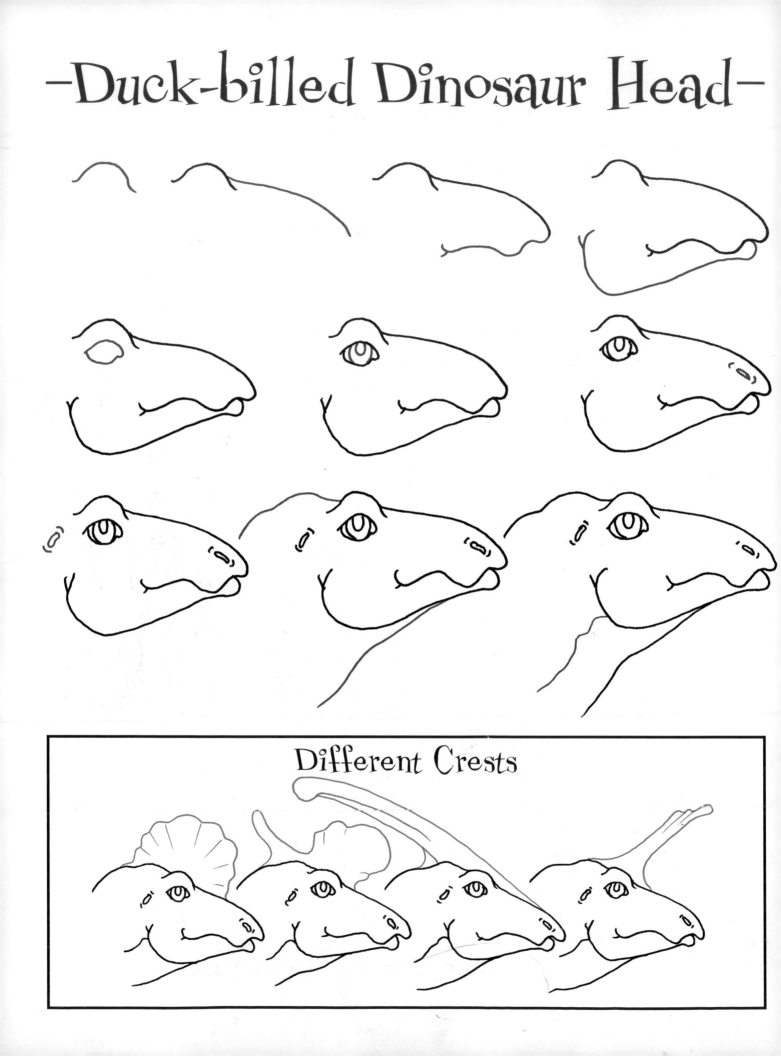

Different Crests

Anyone for ring toss?

watercolor and colored pencil

Duck-billed Body

Choose a head for your duck-billed dinosaur and add some color and pattern.

marker and pastel pencil

Spinosaurus Head

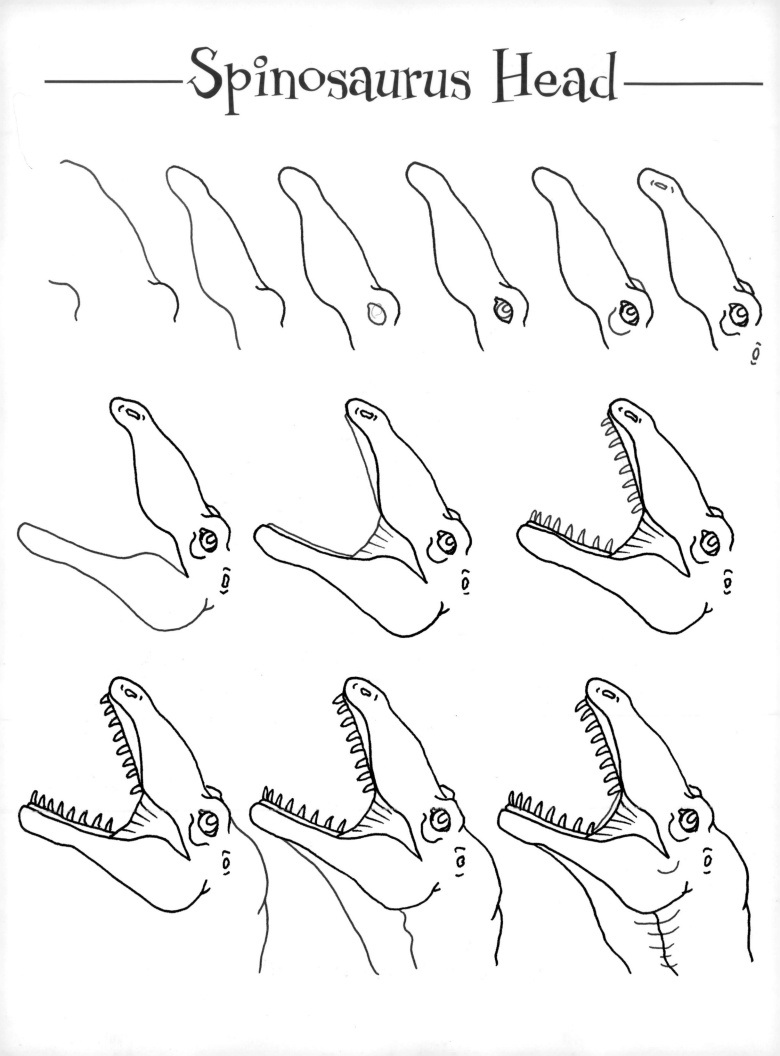

Sink your teeth into drawing.

marker and colored pencil

Spinosaurus Body

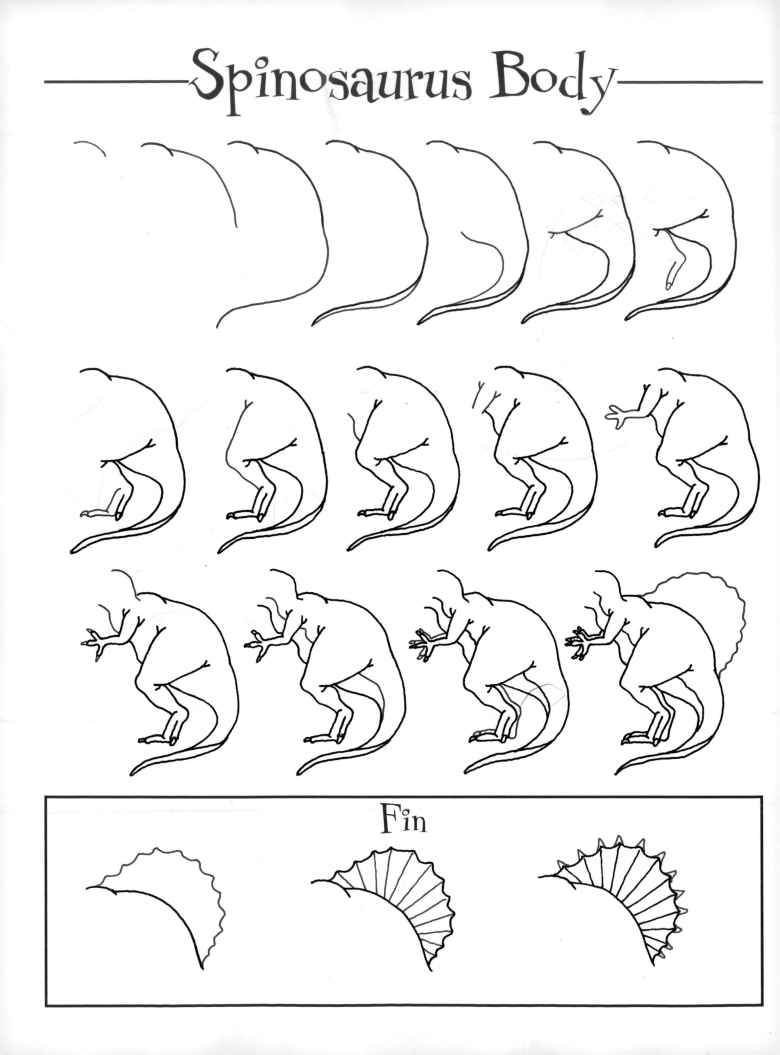

Fin

Going for a sail?

marker and watercolor

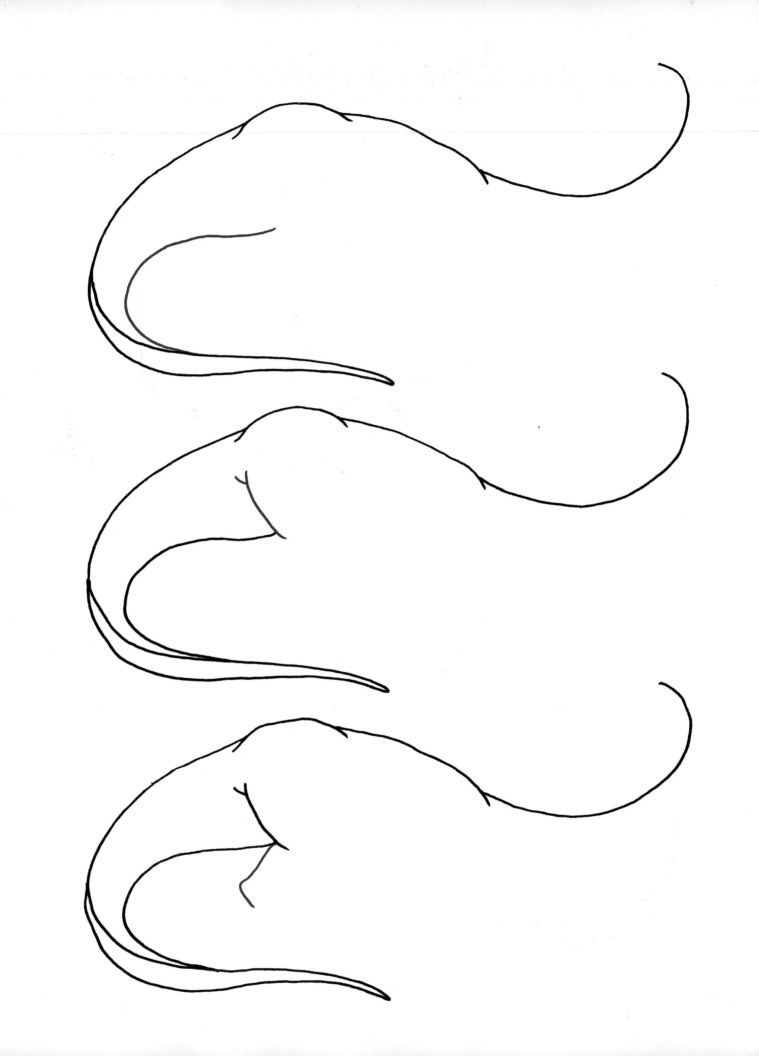

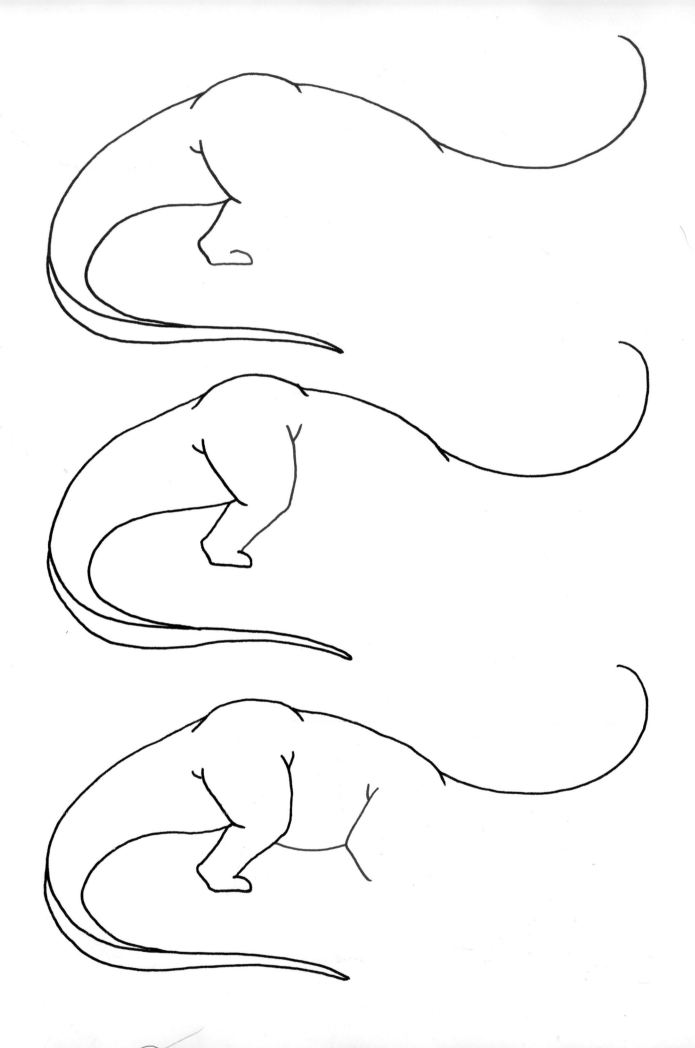

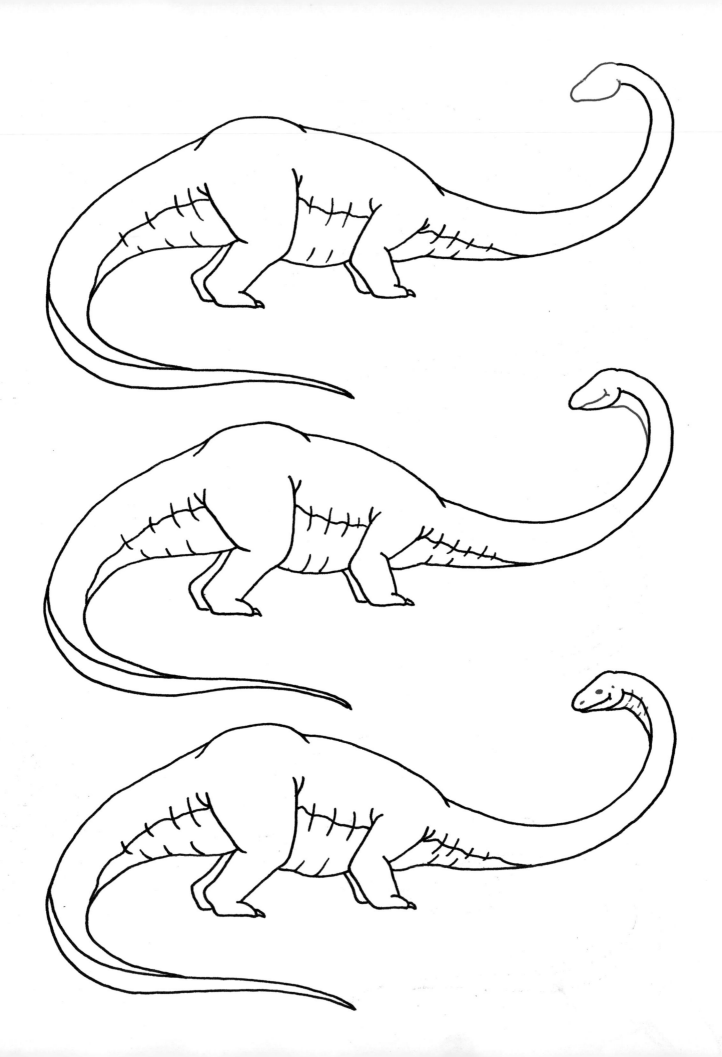

Tyrannosaurus Head

My, what big teeth you have!

marker, pastel pencil, and colored pencil

Tyrannosaurus Body

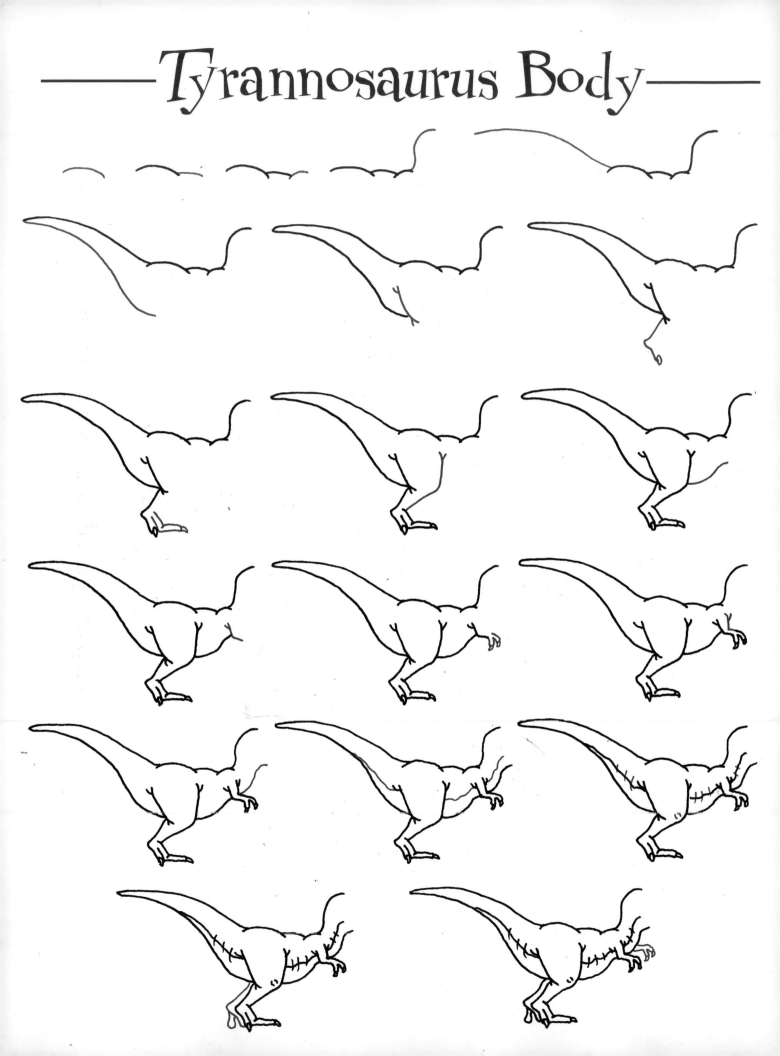

Where's dinner?

marker, pastel pencil, and colored pencil

Now make up your own dino-designs.
What should I name this one?
I'll call it a Ralphasaurus!

Have fun, and keep on drawing!